At the Barber

Published by The Child's World®, Inc.

Design and Production:
The Creative Spark, San Juan Capistrano, CA

Photos: © 1998 David M. Budd Photography
Illustrations: Robert Court

Library of Congress Cataloging-in-Publication Data
Sirimarco, Elizabeth 1966-
      At the barber / by Elizabeth Sirimarco.
         p. cm.
      Summary: A simple introduction to the barber shop or beauty salon, who works
there, what activities are performed in cutting and styling hair, and what tools and
other items are used.
      ISBN 1-56766-571-3 (alk. paper)
      1. Barbering Juvenile literature. 2. Barbershops Juvenile literature. [1. Barbering.
2. Barbershops.] I. Title.
TT957.S57 1999
646.7'24—dc21   99-19551
                                                                                          CIP

At the Barber

Written by Elizabeth Sirimarco
Photos by David M. Budd

The Child's World®, Inc.

Let's get a haircut!

We can visit the barber shop.

Some people call it a beauty salon.

People who cut and **style** hair are

called barbers or stylists.

There are about 700,000 barbers and stylists in the United States!

This customer has an **appointment.**

She tells the worker her name.

The worker checks the barber's **schedule.**

"Oh yes. Here you are," she tells the customer.

I'm here for a haircut, please!

A barber works with many people every day.

Sometimes she works with children.

Some children don't like to cut their hair.

"Don't worry," says the barber.

"We won't take too much off."

9

This little girl only wants a **trim.**
The barber is very careful.

Look how long her hair is!

Some people like their hair best
when it's short.

The barber uses a **clipper.**

The clipper makes a funny noise.

Buzz! Buzz!

Careful! Is the clipper sharp?

The next customer wants his hair
a little longer.

The barber uses scissors to cut his hair.

She makes sure her customers are happy.

This customer wants a special style.
She is going to a party tonight!
The barber makes her hair look pretty.

Some people like to change the color
of their hair.

The barber looks at different colors.

She chooses the best one.

The barber uses **dye** to make the color.

The barber paints the dye on the customer's hair. She only paints a few pieces of hair.

The dye is wet and cold!

She wraps the hair in shiny paper.

The paper keeps the dye in place.

Now the customer waits for a little while.

Yuck! The dye doesn't smell very good.

Now it's time to rinse off the extra dye.

The barber washes the customers hair.

Ahhh. The water is nice and warm.

Mmmmmm. The shampoo smells nice!

"Time to dry your hair!"

The barber uses a **blow dryer.**

Whirrr! Whirrr!

She curls the customer's hair
around a brush.

The barber uses hair spray. Spritz! Spritz!

It helps the hair hold its shape.

What do you think?

"It looks great!" says the customer.

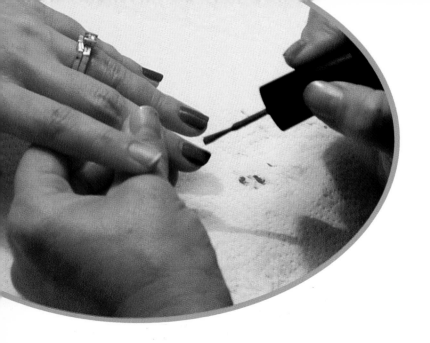

"One more thing before I leave," says the customer. "I'd like to get a **manicure.**" A worker paints the customer's fingernails.

Careful!
Don't spill the polish!

28

29

Now it's time to pay the bill.

The customer makes an

appointment for next time.

See you soon!

Now I'm going to go show
off my new hairstyle!

31

Glossary

appointment (a-POINT-ment) — An appointment is a set time to meet someone. A customer makes an appointment with a barber.

clipper (KLIP-ur) — A clipper is an object used to cut or clip something. Barbers use clippers to cut some people's hair.

dye (DIE) — Dye is a substance that can change the color of something. Barbers use dye to color people's hair.

blow dryer (BLO DRY-ur) — A blow dryer is an electric machine that blows warm air. Barbers use blow dryers to dry people's hair.

manicure (MAN-eh-kyur) — A manicure is a treatment for the hands and fingernails. Some barbers know how to give manicures.

schedule (SKEJ-u-el) — A schedule is a list showing appointment times. A barber has a schedule of appointments.

style (STY-l) — When you style something, you make it look nice. A barber styles hair. Also, the design of a person's hair is called a style.

trim (TRIM) — If you trim something, you cut a small amount of it. Barbers trim people's hair to make it neat.

Index

32

Elizabeth Sirimarco has written more than 20 books for young readers. She and her husband, photographer David Budd, live in Colorado.